T0302778

The God of This World to His Prophet

The God of
This World
to His Prophet

POEMS

Bill Coyle

WINNER OF THE NEW CRITERION POETRY PRIZE

Ivan R. Dee

CHICAGO 2006

For my Family,
especially Mildred Bradley (1902–2002).
May her memory be eternal.

Funding for this year's New Criterion Poetry Prize
has been provided by the Drue Heinz Trust.

THE GOD OF THIS WORLD TO HIS PROPHET. Copyright © 2006 by
Bill Coyle. All rights reserved, including the right to reproduce this
book or portions thereof in any form. For information, address:
Ivan R. Dee, Publisher, 1332 North Halsted Street, Chicago 60622.
Manufactured in the United States of America and printed on
acid-free paper.

www.ivanrdee.com

Library of Congress Cataloging-in-Publication Data:
Coyle, Bill, 1968–
    The god of this world to his prophet : poems / Bill Coyle.
    p. cm. — (New Criterion Poetry Prize winners)
    "Winner of the New Criterion Poetry Prize."
    ISBN-13: 978-1-56663-710-7 (cloth : acid-free paper)
    ISBN-10: 1-56663-710-4 (cloth : acid-free paper)
    I. Title.
PS3603.O93G63 2006
811'.6—dc22
                                    2006023670

Contents

The God of This World to His Prophet

The God of This World to His Prophet

Go to the prosperous city,
for I have taken pity

on its inhabitants,
who drink and feast and dance

all night in lighted halls
yet know their bacchanals

lead nowhere in the end.
Go to them, now, commend,

to those with ears to hear,
a lifestyle more austere.

Tell all my children tired
of happiness desired

and never had that there
is solace in despair.

Say there is consolation
in ruins and ruination

beneath a harvest moon
that is itself a ruin,

comfort, however cold,
in grievances recalled

beside a fire dying
from lack of love and trying.

Tjelvars Grav

Gotland, Sweden

It is a chilly day in late December.
The ground is dusted lightly over with snow.
The sun goes down at three, casting a glow
that freezes each particular in amber.
We shiver while we watch the last light go.

We note the sounds of passing traffic, brief
sighs, like the wind, brief stops of silence. Here,
just off the road a bit, where the trees clear,
a stone ship built to ply the afterlife
weathers the elements, year after year.

Here is the life-sized, dirt-floored hull of stones
so worn one half imagines it has been
to death's uncharted shore and back again.
Here, a plaque informs us, lay the bones
of an anonymous, seafaring man.

Tjelvar, the local legends call him, giving
to undistinguished bronze-age bones the name
of the apocryphal first man who came
to Gotland at the dawn of time. The living,
as always, are preoccupied with fame,

which is a kind of immortality,
though not, to judge from this, the concrete kind
Tjelvar (what else to call him?) had in mind.
Adrift on the unfathomable sea,
what was it he imagined he would find?

Lawrence saw vividly the new life's dawn.
Did Tjelvar see it, does he see it now,
staring intently from his stone ship's bow?
Or does he, in the dark, continue on,
drifting wherever wind and wave allow?

Or has he—I can hardly bear the thought—
dispassionately let his stone ship sink?
Did he slip under softly, did he drink
that dead sea's nothingness till he was not?
I am uncertain, finally, what to think.

I am unable, finally, to decide
if faith is more than one more way of trying
to make the factual less terrifying.
Tjelvar, if he ever lived, died.
A pair of gulls wheel overhead, crying.

Leave Taking

i.m. Sten Söderström

The dead, we say, are the departed. They
pass on, they pass away, they leave behind
family, friends, the whole of humankind—
they have gone on before. Or so we say.

But could it be the opposite is true?
Now, as I stand here in the graveled drive
at moonrise, unaccountably alive,
I have the sense that it is we, not you,

who are departing, spun at breakneck speed
through space and time, while you stay where you are—
intimate of dark matter and bright star—
and watch the brilliant, faithless world recede.

Living

In winter, once the ice on the lake is safe,
a group of local ice-fishers build a town
    with houses, streets, a store, a tavern—
        all the necessities—then move out there.

By day they wait for nothing they sense or see
until a line goes taut like a sudden thought,
    and someone lifts a flash of silver
        out of an opening in the surface.

With darkness, things are otherwise. Then the lights
that glitter on the shore they have left behind
    amount to a new constellation
        born in the lowliest part of heaven;

then sometime neighbors head to their tavern, where,
because they know the season is all too brief,
    they stay up later than they mean to,
        playing guitar, trading stories, drinking,

and feeling how expansive it strangely is
to have it all come down to this makeshift town
    then, closer, to this point, this tavern
        crowded with music and light and voices.

Past closing, now. The bartender, bound for what,
for the time being, is home, recollects the stars.
    Out of a pocket near his heart he
        fishes a flask of the local moonshine.

There is a dark below and a dark above;
the fish are darting stars, while the stars are schools
    that drift so glacially their slightest
        movement plays out over generations.

It is a private vision. Around him sleep
his customers and friends in their home-spun homes.
    He takes a measured swig of liquor,
        grimaces, grins. It is nearly daybreak.

The Magic Circle

1. Autumn

Early this morning I glanced out the window
and saw her underneath the maple tree.
She was as pale as that white gown of hers.
Hard to believe it's been a year already.
I waved. She turned away, paused for a moment,
then walked into the mist that marked the border
between my backyard and what lay beyond.
Proserpine, I called, but she was gone.
I am convinced that this was Proserpine
and not, as Mrs. Grandison maintains,
some nut escaped from the state hospital.
All Hallow E'en approaches. Skeletons
hang from the trees along my street and ghosts,
emboldened, haunt the front yards in broad daylight.

2. Winter

The swallows sleep beneath the river ice.
The salamanders whisper in the fire.
Hermes Trismestigus' new work is open
at one of its obscurer passages,
of which there are intolerably many.
I take a break to watch the local news.

Toward midnight, I collect my charts and go
to make my nightly survey of the heavens.
Mercifully they're still there. One of the saddest
developments I've witnessed in my time
has been astrology's decline from science
to fortune telling of the basest sort,
its long eclipse by disciplines that measure
not meaning, now, but distance, size and mass . . .
As if mere matter mattered in itself.

3. Spring

Bears wake from their long hibernation, now,
hirsute initiates with tales to tell
to those with ears to listen. Proserpine
returns as well, and Christ. And may not I?
The budding trees and the returning birds
figure the transmigration of the soul
so beautifully I wish that I could die
and see the world again through infant eyes.
I intimate these things to Ed, my mailman,
who nods politely. Ed is not about
to jeopardize his Christmas tip (last year
an old tin can transmuted into gold)
regardless how much of a character
he and the other villagers may think me.

4. Summer

Little did I know when I concocted
my potion that, although one may stop time,
it is impossible to turn it back.
Youth, they say, is wasted on the young.

Perhaps I'll have a tee-shirt made that reads,
Eternal life is wasted on the old.
And yet the world is no less beautiful.
Toward evening dew collects upon the lawn,
rising again as fireflies. Above
the white New England church a flock of swallows
copies a Greek text out in Arabic,
and in the maple trees a light breeze stirs,
sounding for all the world like water falling
distantly off the edges of the world.

Strawberries

I do not believe in the fox that comes
stealing between the close-knit pines,
he is perfection, and, as such, beyond me;

he comes, nonetheless, at nightfall, quiet,
all but silent, quiet as
spiritus in the pines, say, or this moonrise,

comes through the cooling grass, the garden,
bows or assumes his hunting posture
in going past our statue of St. Francis,

poor Francis, with both hands extended,
the right to bless, the left to beg,
the Lord giveth, and the Lord taketh away . . .

I am picking wild strawberries when he comes,
my fingertips and lips incarnadine,
the taste already fading on my tongue.

Regret

How to explain?
The wind sighs in the trees,
leafing through memories
of last night's rain.

Abandoned Bridges

You've seen them in the countryside
now and again, abandoned bridges
standing a stone's throw from the roads
that passed them by decades before.
Always you have driven past
and thought to stop but had no time.

Today, though, you have made the time.
You have pulled over to the side,
letting the other cars stream past,
and stopped at one of these old bridges,
just as you should have done before,
on other days and other roads.

Should have. And yet those other roads
seemed to promise at the time
some miracle not seen before.
How could you pause, then, at the side?
And what, you reasoned, were those bridges
but relics of the recent past?

It took you years to love the past,
you who believed in open roads
and had no use for useless bridges.
Once you even thought that time,

impartial time, was on your side.
You were oblivious before.

Not now. Now, as you stand before
this bridge and contemplate the past,
you feel a perfect peace inside.
Let others speed by on the roads.
You could pass happily the time
admiring abandoned bridges.

For now you fathom how these bridges,
as needful as they were before,
only grow more so over time,
how they lead us to a past
inaccessible by roads.
You look toward the other side.

There, on the other side of time,
the past waits as it did before
we came and built our roads and bridges.

Cosmos

Moscow I remember
as grey streets, grey buildings, grey skies.
This was in February,
which can't have helped matters.

But I remember too
how, across the way
from the Hotel Cosmos,
by the Astronautic Museum,

a jet-trail of titanium
red in the setting sun
rose, arced and narrowed
to a little silver spacecraft,

and how, in the dark beneath
the city, between palatial,
tiled and chandeliered stations,
the subway trains flew.

Anno Domini

Consider the ravens: for they neither sow
nor reap; which neither have storehouse nor barn . . .
So Jesus, far away and long ago,
instructed his friends in holy unconcern.

They mustn't have had squirrels in Palestine
(note to self: look this up). In any case,
he omitted them—their clutching sense of *mine*,
mine being obviously out of place.

I like to sit here watching the local squirrels,
the way they gather nuts, bury them, hide
the spot with dirt and twigs, the way their quarrels
chase them around and up a maple's side,

The way that they come closer when I call,
and even when I don't—the way they stand
begging—year-round but more so in the fall—
prepared to take the food right from my hand.

One will eat each nut as it's doled out;
another will eat one and bury two;
another takes a nibble of each nut,
pauses and considers what to do.

Consider the squirrels of the park, they gather
their nuts and steal their neighbor's when they can.
Their plumpness presages the colder weather.
What careful, small, grey creatures. How like man.

When common sense requires that we fill
our stores against the time of scarcity,
how can He tell us in good conscience, *fool,*
this night thy soul shall be required of thee?

Treasure in heaven? Closer at hand, the ravens
stalk glassy eyed through leaves of fallen gold,
and homeless men lie sprawled out under heaven's
immense capacity for rain and cold.

Disaster

All do not all things well,
and there are few things more
thankless than trying to tell
a friend he hasn't got
an ounce of talent for
the work nearest his heart—
which is why I was not
straight with you from the start.

An asteroid on a course
for earth, caught early enough
could, with a hint of force
(and a good dose of math)
be steered fatefully off.
Once, a word to you
might have changed your path.
Now what can I do?

Now it is too late:
now the course you've chosen
has all the force of fate,
and if I pointed out
you're bound for a collision
with the reality
of who you are, I doubt
you'd hear me, or agree.

You are both asteroid
and shadowed impact zone
and neither can avoid
the crash that's on its way;
and I, who might have known—
who knew—how this would end
am not about to say
anything now, my friend.

Bitters

Ash Wednesday

I'm urged to *turn away from sin and follow*
the Gospel. Gracious words, yet they ring hollow
without that stem reminder I am dust.
Well, God remembers what I am, I trust.

Epitaph for a Philosopher

He has become, in Death, the dust that yields
the harvest of uncounted killing fields.

Loser's Lament

I learned this early on: no pain, no gain.
A pity the reverse does not obtain.

Dark

Drinking a dark beer in a darker mood
I fantasize the perfect solitude:
another full pint of this bitter beer
and nobody, myself included, here.

Commentary on Ecclesiastes

Everything's been done to death?
Then saying so's a waste of breath.

Friend, in the desolate hour . . .

from the Swedish of Erik Johan Stagnelius

Friend, in the desolate hour, when your soul is enshrouded in darkness,
    When, in a deep abyss, memory and sense disappear,
Intellect timidly gropes among shadowy forms and illusions
    Heart can no longer sigh, eye is unable to weep;
When, from your night-clouded soul the wings of fire have fallen,
    And you feel yourself sink, fearful, to nothing again,
Say, who rescues you then? — Who is the comforting angel
    That gives your inner self order and beauty again,
Building once more your fragmented world, restoring the fallen
    Altar, and when it is raised, lighting the sacred flame? —
None but the powerful being who first from the limitless darkness
    Kissed to life seraphs and woke numberless suns to their dance.
None but the holy Word that cried to the worlds, "Ye shall be . . . "
    And in whose power the worlds move on their paths even now.
Therefore, rejoice, oh friend, and sing in the darkness of sorrow:
    Night is the mother of day, Chaos the neighbor of God.

Trinitarian

The World is a rebellious child at play,
watched by its anxious parents Night and Day.

*

The Flesh, regardless of what Christ might say,
is willing. Any time of night or day.

*

The Devil is Our Father, and so we pray
to have tomorrow's bread today. Today.

The Common

I.

Now, when the trees are bare, I can see in their upper branches
        nests that the birds of the air built for themselves and their young.
These do not sow or reap or store up in barns, yet their dwellings
        seem to me to surpass anything I could make.
Why are they worth less than I, then? And where is the human spirit?
        Where, if not in the wind stirring the branches now?

2.

Once I detested the look of skeletal branches in winter;
        now I am ready to learn all that they have to teach,
ready to turn from the evergreen trees that have been through the ages
        types of eternal life, green and full all year round.
Christ, give me life everlasting, but give me, to guide me in this life,
        trees that put forth their leaves, lose them, then grow them again.

3.

Out on the common the leafless boughs have been decked out for
    months, now,
        strings of white Christmas tree lights twined around each bare limb.
Every tree, by night, is a branch of Yggdrasil, world-tree
        ramifying its way into the darkness of space.
Artifice, at its heart, is the human touch describing
        lucidly what the world, stripped to its essence, is.

Airports: An Ode

for Michael Lind

If the poetic line,
  as seems to be the case, is
 that there could not be any less
   poetic places
 than major airports, then I guess
I ought in all good conscience to resign
my membership in the great brotherhood,
since I can't help but think these places good.

Granted, the meals are bland
  (though laughably expensive)
 the travelers bored beyond belief
   (though apprehensive);
 granted, a soul might come to grief
(and many have) trying to understand
a given airport's kabalistic maze.
Still, these are places worthy of our praise,

worthy because in fact they are
a means by which we realize
the ancient dream of humankind:
not just to travel fast and far
but to ascend into the skies
and, living, leave the world behind.

And if the terminals,
   their faults being so apparent,
seem lowly means to that high end,
    that's still no warrant
for purist bards to condescend.
Let them remember that within these walls,
among kitsch art and commerce, we await
translation to that other, higher state.

   Let them remember, too,
    that air travel, however
standardized it has grown, remains
    a bold endeavor:
Safe though they are as houses, planes
crash upon take-off, plummet from the blue
or serve as flying bombs in an assault.
So let the poets leave off finding fault;

let them, as is meet and right,
recall how, in antiquity,
that engineer extraordinaire,
father of Icarus and flight,
arrived bereft in Italy.
What he did once we daily dare.

Traveling Alone

Fetching a luggage wagon, I'm aware,
not for the first time on this journey, how
bizarre it is for me that you're not here,
that I can't turn and talk to you just now.

I know I shouldn't over-dramatize;
it's only going to mean a week away.
It isn't even, I now realize,
as if I'd anything that much to say,

aside from *I'll go grab a wagon*, which,
if you were here, you would assume I'd do.
And yet the fact that I can't mumble such
a consummate banality to you

and hear your equally mundane *all right*
makes me feel shut up inside my skin.
Nothing, not the others from the flight
shouldering for their baggage, nor the din

of intercom and small talk reaches me
(being neither here nor there) where I
am lost in thought, thinking how it will be
if you should be the first of us to die.

One Flesh

for Cattie

Toweling off I look out through
    the bathroom doorway to
a mirror hanging on the wall
    across the narrow hall,
and, from this angle, see instead
    of me, you. Fresh from bed,
eyes shut, head back, you stand and stretch,
    not seeing how I watch,
modestly unaware how I
    find myself taken by
(after ten years of love, no less)
    your naked otherness.
I stand and let my vision go
    over your body in slow
motion — toe to head to toe.
    I know, love, what I know:
Flesh of my flesh, I know as time
    passes, that we two rhyme
more perfectly. Bone of my bone,
    neither of us alone
could be the incarnation of
    the pattern of our love.

Now, in the mirror, I see you,
  eyes open, look out through
the bedroom doorway, see you see,
  in the same mirror, me.
You wave and I wave back, we laugh.
  Good morning, better half.

Knowledge

Knowledge is found at the Know Ledge,
high above all you know
and when you stand there scanning
the world below,

it won't, for all its beauty,
be the phenomenal view
of foreign and familiar
that dazzles you—

mountains on the horizon
staggering toward the sun,
the flood-plains where your battles
were lost and won—

But how, when you stand on the Know Ledge,
and catch your breath and call
to the world you came from, crying
hello to it all,

you hear within the voices
echoing in reply
an emptiness allowing
for earth and sky.

The Face on Mars

a sermon

Friends, it is good to see you here today,
good to have had this time with you to pray.
Please, please. Be seated. What I have to say,

though new to everybody here, will not,
I think, shock you, for everything I've taught,
the whole evolving system of my thought,

has led me (it is clear in retrospect)
to this: a truth the whole world will reject—
except for you, my dear ones, my elect.

You will recall, from past sermons I've given
on different members of the host of heaven,
that Mars is the most crucial—more so even

than Jupiter. I wonder have you read
any of what has recently been said
about Mars having been inhabited?

Some of these people are lunatics, I know.
Others are careful, sober thinkers, though,
and they have photographs that they say show,

there, in the highlands of that desert place,
the outlines of a faintly human face
staring, lips parted slightly, into space.

Having made out its outlines, they are prone
to see there proof of what they've always known —
that we are not — or once were not — alone.

In their imaginations cities rise,
splendid, spindly into Martian skies.
Then, over time, that civilization dies

down into rust-red ruins, killed no doubt
by slow asphyxiation and by drought
as atmosphere and water are leaked out

Into the void.
                    Most experts, of course, dismiss
the face-as-artifact hypothesis,
claiming that so-called artifacts like this

are shadows and eroded stone combined
by sharp eyes and an overactive mind.
Looking at the same photos, they can find

or say that they can find — no evidence
of cities or canals or monuments —
in short, no sure signs of intelligence.

Whom to believe, then? True believers who
insist their tales of aliens are true
or cold skeptics who take the other view?

Neither, for neither faction understands
the truth—that the face rising from red sands
is genuine, but was not made by hands

or by the action of the Martian weather
but by a third force, different altogether .
It is on Mars, you see, that our dead gather—

being well-suited to existence there—
and that enormous face with vacant stare
is the collective mask of stone they wear.

Ah, how contemplative they are, how far
from all the suffering in our blue star.
Would that we were as peaceful as they are!

Would that we literally could rise above
the dualistic world of hate and love.
Ah, but we can. It's purely a matter of

finding the proper mode of transportation.
This, after days of contemplation,
I have done. Friends, I can sense your anticipation.

Pills are being given out to all of you,
and if you want to—friends, I know you do—
we can go now. All that I've said is true:

I know where the dead are, and you and I
can join them. No, there is no need to fly.
The only thing we need to do is die.

Godhood

from the Swedish of Bertil Malmberg

I.

It struck me always as odd
that anyone could love
the distant, omnipotent God
we enthroned above.
Though it was thought that he
is as mild as glorious,
still, he meant less to me
than a destitute mother does.
None but a human soul
can warm my own,
none but a soul that has known
corruption's toll,
none but the being that despairs,
captive in suffering's ring
—none but the heart that bears
all manner of baffling thing,
some of it folly, and some
dark wisdom, upon reflection.
—How could one ever come
to love perfection?

II.

The heart feels nothing for your power, no,
and nothing for the princes who
in legions throng your court to worship you.
High emptinesses from your mantle flow.

You are, were, and shall be the God of might,
and by your will's command and choice you lead
the constellations of the year and write
the secrets of the ages overhead.

So scripture and tradition both attest.
But it may be that you are more
removed from the stern image some adore
than is the north from south, or east from west.

From absolutist rule of time and space,
from lonely majesty no good can come.
If cloudless glory is you royal home
I neither want, nor pray to have, your grace.

But if you are powerless, one eternally
with all that wanders, hunts, and dies and dies,
and should this unity comprise
your godhood and your immortality;

and if you are the voice that strains to speak
in wind and rain and in the anxiousness
of frightened hands as they caress
a loved one's pale, almost transparent cheek;

and if you reconcile, as is my hope,
time, love, decay, and groanings of despair—
then it is after you I grope
and you, my God, whom I seek everywhere.

III.

Godhood that hunts and slays,
shadowy, on the run,
—while the centuries, brief as days,
like tatters and leaves are spun

—to me you seem
an unending woe:
now like a wandering gleam,
now like a howling you go.

You are the wild
the obscure
that brushes by
Yes, you are the longing and cry—
but also the ever mild
the ever secure . . .

In your poverty's miserable cliff
where the chill winds sniff
where the rain and mist never cease
and the bats huddle close to each other,
there the soul rests in nameless peace
—however the fates protest—
as the little ones rest
with the she-wolf, their mother.

Perspectives

i.

Hardy, in his great poem "Hap," maintains
he would be comforted to find his pains

were not what they in fact appear to be —
expected outcomes of "Crass Casualty" —

but the fulfillment of some higher will
intent on doing Thomas Hardy ill.

ii.

Aeneas, faced with overwhelming odds,
saw in a vision how the very gods

whom he had served now helped his foes destroy
the walls and towers and palaces of Troy.

There is in Virgil, though, no evidence
this vision comforted the Trojan prince.

Fallen

Crabapple blossoms, blown,
fall and flutter down,

littering like confetti
the main street of our city.

Confetti . . . the simile
quickens, and you and I,

walking sometime later
amidst the drifted litter

come to realize
that we feel ill at ease

in this belated beauty
since, if it is confetti,

it means that we have missed
some great thing seen by most:

Say that we did; what was it?
Some dignitary's visit?

Some holiday parade
or hometown hero's ride?

Something in us cautions
against the kind of questions

that now come welling up
but which we cannot stop:

If there was a celebration,
what was the occasion,

and why did we not know
about it until now?

We read the daily papers;
we chatted with our neighbors

and friends and relatives.
We've lived here all our lives,

but if we are no longer
at home here, should we linger?

Where can we turn, and to whom,
if this is not our home?

The Language of Birds

Years ago, on a trip to Gothenburg,
(or *Göteborg*, as it's called in Swedish)
as we were touring the Botanic Gardens,
a voice came from on high saying *hej på dig*!—
Swedish for *hi there*—with the local accent.
It was a bright red parrot on a branch.
We stopped and chatted with him—*Hej på dig
Vad heter du? Vad kan du säga annars?
Hi there. What's your name? What else can you say?*—
eventually concluding *hej på dig*
must be his one phrase. Then, as we turned to go,
he spoke back up, saying *hej då, goodbye*.

Alarmists—and I guess I'm one of them—
point with, what else, alarm, to inroads English
has made into the smaller European
languages, Swedish being an example,
point to the English language shows and films
(*subtitled almost for appearance's sake*),
the advertisements (*Levi's billed as being
"Born in the USA"*), the countless loan-words
(*yes, party, TV, talk show, e-mail, weekend*) . . .
Our friend, though, lived in blissful ignorance

of any sociolinguistic changes
happening in the world beyond the glass,
through which he saw but darkly, if at all.

2.

One of the reports of Eden tells
how in the garden, before the fall of Man,
people and animals spoke the same language.
Parrots even now, another says,
speak it, though we no longer understand it.
Is it nostalgia for those times that makes us
suckers for tales where animals can talk,
that makes us talk to animals like children,
that makes some people want to keep a parrot?
Or is it just the charm of hearing our words,
even the most banal, repeated back
like mantras, or the clauses of a creed?

I've heard of one, for instance, whose vocabulary
and sense of context were so far advanced
that anytime somebody would come in
shivering and complaining about the cold
it would pipe up with, "Would you like some soup?"
Or when a thunder storm panicked the dog
assured him, "It's okay, it's okay."
It couldn't actually prepare the soup,
but it was such good company for the dog
that when a storm did come, the dog would run
and slump down underneath the parrot's cage
to listen till the weather had blown over
to "It's okay, it's okay, it's okay."

Nobody who grew up on Monty Python
can think for very long of the word "parrot"
and not recall the great "Dead Parrot Sketch,"
in which a man discovers that the parrot
he bought "not a half an hour before" is dead,
and goes back to the pet store to complain.
Most of the ensuing sketch he spends
trying to get the shop clerk to admit
the parrot is, in point of fact, dead,
and not, to name just two alternatives
the clerk in desperation hits upon,
"shagged out after a long squall" or—given
that the dead bird was a "Norwegian Blue"—
"pining for the fjords." The sketch's highpoint
comes when the customer, at his wit's end,
and at the end of an interminable
harangue in which he runs through nearly every
imaginable way to say "he's dead,"
exclaims—at this point he is almost screeching—
'e's shuffled off this mortal coil, run down
the curtain and joined the bleedin' choir invisibile!!
THIS IS AN EX-PARROT!! Whereupon,
finally, the clerk admits the parrot's dead,
and since he hasn't got one to replace it,
offers the customer a slug instead:

"Pray, can it talk?" the customer demands.
"Not really, no," the clerk replies, abashed.
"Well then, it's hardly a replacement, is it?"

4.

Maybe they have a language of their own, though,
the rudiments of one, at any rate.
Researchers have discovered that, in some
species, each bird within a given flock
has a specific call it calls its own
and will respond to when another parrot
or a researcher who has prerecorded
the call as uttered by some other parrot,
uses it. Some, in other words, have names.

Adam gave names to all the animals
and then to Eve, when she came on the scene,
but when he first woke out of nonexistence,
he had no name himself and, having none,
scarcely even knew he was a self.
It was a parrot seated in a tree
who first suggested, maybe jokingly,
that the new animal should be named Adam,
after the earth from which he had been formed.

5.

There are the colors, which can leave you speechless —
garish on shirts with tropical motifs,
and often, even on the birds themselves,
so, well, electric I'm inclined to wonder
if the whole march of mankind from whatever
son of Cain invented engineering
down to Thomas Alva Edison
can't be construed as an unconscious effort
to make lights bright enough that they'd provide

an adjective to modify these colors,
these reds and greens and blues, oranges, yellows . . .
Not surprisingly, the Norwegian Blue
hasn't been sighted outside that one sketch
in 1969, but if it were,
it would be fjord blue, I'm certain of it,
blue as deep, near arctic water, save
for legs and claws of life-preserver orange.

Nomadic by nature, the Norwegian Blue
would fly from fjord to fjord, gathering up
words from each village's local dialect,
like a winged linguist, like the two men who,
when National Romanticism ruled,
tramped through the countryside recording folktales,
twisting the syntax of their schoolroom Danish,
taking down words that otherwise would vanish,
their motto a pre-modern "make it old,"
the end result what we call New Norwegian.

6.

Apparently, the last surviving speaker
of Cornish was—I kid you not—a parrot.
Poor creature. What a burden those few phrases,
parroted back ad infinitum were.
Taken to London, he spent his last years
lecturing at the Royal Academy
while linguists tried in vain to reconstruct
a basic grammar of his dying tongue.
Happier to imagine him translated
into the Paradise of talking birds:
There, in every tree, a brilliant parrot

fluent in some no longer human tongue—
Cornish, Umbrian, Thracian, Avestan—
and versed in all its poetry and prose
is holding forth for benefit of pilgrims
bound for the heart of that untended garden.

There, in the branches of the Tree of Life
one parrot, beautiful beyond belief,
perches and preaches in what is,
if now incomprehensible to us,
nevertheless the language of our first
parents and each succeeding generation
(though it grew more corrupted over time)
down to the tower and that divine confusion.

The Flautist of North Station

The flautist of North Station,
playing "Amazing Grace,"
will get, for compensation,
some quarters in a case

on which, for sympathy,
he's taped a picture of
his daughters, so that we
may see he plays for love;

may see he plays for free,
while someone in a suit
takes up the melody
our man plays on the flute

and starts to whistle it
as he departs the station,
bound for a world unfit
for any such salvation.

The Man in the Moon

No, he is not Cain, wandering still in exile,
dogged by a dog we take to be "the foul
fiend" incognito, burdened with a thornbush
emblematic of the thorns that grew
in answer to God's curse on our first parents . . .

No, he is not Endymion, that shepherd-
prince whom the goddess of the moon so loved
she took him up into her dwelling, where
he lives on, now immortal and the doting
father of some fifty demigoddesses . . .

No, but he is a small grey man—grey hair,
grey eyes, grey trenchcoat buttoned to the top—
who blends chameleon-like into the moonscape.
The type who, had he lived among us, surely
would have been no-one or a master spy.

He lives alone here in a little crater
left on the shoreline of the Sea of Storms,
the roof that he will never build his shelter,
the stones he gathers every day his bread,
the gathering of stones his occupation.

This is the kind of life that he was born to.
He finds it hard to imagine any other,
and when he thinks of us, it is with pity.
How, he wonders, can we bear to live
where there is still so much left to be lost?

Here he sits watching wave on non-existent
wave break on beaches that do not decay,
counting above him in the darkness stars
that do not flicker (like our own) like candles—
though they are burning just as surely down.

Myself

What should I bring? Just yourself, they assure me. Which, granted,
    is nice, but . . .
        Jesus. What if I did? How could I live it down?
Give him an hour, he'd be drunk off his ass, critiquing the husband,
        openly groping the wife, ruining priceless antiques,
looking for fights with the others, then taking offense when challenged . . .
        Self will be staying at home. Maybe I'll bring a bouquet.

A Bubble Burst

Groggy with sleep this morning
I somehow thought
Ness meant Lake in Scottish —
which it does *not*

and thinking I had a poem —
or the end of one —
I paused from doing dishes
to jot down

not much — two lines — but welcome
after so long,
only, an instant later,
to see I'd been wrong.

Back at the dishes, clearer-
headed, my dream
of something great submerging
in suds and steam,

I cling to the lines; they're catchy,
if meaningless,
and nothing breaks the surface
of Nothing Ness.

Table Talk

It was a meeting of two modern masters
when Groucho Marx and T. S. Eliot,
mutual admirers, sat down to dinner,
but brilliant conversation it was not.

Each man, it seems, was too in awe of the other,
Eliot eager to demonstrate that he
knew scores of Groucho's jokes by heart and Groucho
that he was versed in Eliot's poetry.

Still, I'd give anything to hear them chatting.
Groucho, with perfect seriousness would say,
"Who is the third who always walks beside you?"
and Eliot, laughing, "if I could walk *that* way . . ."

Research and Development

The king, reminded he put on his pants
exactly like the general population,
consulted with his royal sycophants
on how to remedy the situation.
For decades, then, sustained by royal grants
(funded in turn by ruinous taxation)
the nation's brightest minds toiled on like ants.
It very nearly bankrupted the nation.
And there were some who thought his highness mad,
and ridiculed his project as mere folly
(still others thought his wastefulness a crime)
but in the end his aging highness had
a cross between a harness and a pulley
that lowered him in *both* legs at a time.

Freud's Dog

The Doctor, seated at his desk, has turned
to watch his dog, a little chow-chow who
stands gazing up, visibly concerned,
past the photographer, through time, at you.
That tensed body, that cocked head, that soft gaze
in lieu of language make his feelings known.
Fear, curiosity, desire for praise—
you recognize the feelings as your own.
For both of you are motivated by
such drives, such biologic absolutes,
as reason cannot comfortably control,
and looking in those eyes, now, you see why
in mongrel English the linguistic roots
of *Animal* and *Psyche* both mean Soul.

Anima

One of those dismal, end-of-autumn nights
I came around a bend and saw her there,
standing beside the road as though my lights
had conjured her from dark, rain-ridden air.
Twenty years old at most, slender, frail,
she stood with shoulders hunched against the rain,
her black hair pulled back in a ponytail,
her face a mask of disbelief and pain.
Poor soul . . . I knew exactly who she was
and thought of stopping there to help her when
she vanished suddenly, no doubt because
she knew I doubted she had ever been
anything more than my imaginings
projected on a darkened world of things.

Time of Departure

for Lennart Karlsson

The mildest spell of weather since September—
A beach day, crowed the TV weathermen,
the warmest March anyone can remember—
ends, and it's dead of winter once again.
By three o'clock, the skies have turned so somber
(color of ashes, suitable for Lent)
we've lost our fledgling faith in spring and summer,
lost faith as well in all they might have meant.
Father, permit that we of little faith
may trust in things as basic as the seasons,
the busy sky above, the love of friends.
Ensure that this, that all our goings forth,
offer themselves as suitable occasions
to praise the Love on which this world depends.

Sleeper

The signal might come any time, they said,
adding that he would know it when it came.
He dreams of it while lying awake in bed:
a phone call, someone whispering his real name.
Then the instructions: where to go, and when,
what to do when he gets there, and to whom.
Then the resulting revolution, then,
at long last, his return in triumph home.
How desperately he cherishes the sense
(fading now) of being set above,
by virtue of his special circumstance,
the very people he pretends to love,
any of whom, on any given day,
he would be more than willing to betray.

Episodes

America

He's stopped at an abandoned service station
next to a vacant road in the Southwest.
Fishing a pack of Winstons from his vest,
he lights one, spreads a map, checks his location.
You the viewer have already guessed
that here, beyond the veil of civilization,
he will be put to some dramatic test.

England

His car, sleek as those spaceships on the covers
of science fiction mags from days of yore,
purrs as he puts the pedal to the floor.
Down darkened, cottaged byways he maneuvers,
coolly evading spies or smugglers or . . .
But then you see it: there in his rear-view hovers
a ring of lights around a pulsing core.

The Continent

A distant *au revoir*, then, on the landing.
The waiting, now, bathed in the pool's blue glow.
The grounds, space being scarce, are modest, though

the house itself is vast, with a commanding
view of the starry city spread below.
He and the Countess have an understanding:
he'll slip back in when all the others go.

The Far East

Separated from his expedition,
lost in a blizzard in the mountains, he
is welcomed in by a community
of monks who are, according to tradition,
only a legend from antiquity.
One of them sees in him—not quite contrition,
no—but something no one else can see.

Spring: The Star Magnolia

Wind stirs the branches and white petals fall,
filling the fountain, carpeting the lawn.
The snows of yesteryear have been and gone
and drift the ground in memory, if at all.

Baltic

i.

Before it was inhabited, this island rose
from the sea each morning, then sank each night—
or so the saga has it; it was only
when the first man landed on the shore and lit
a fire there that the spell was broken.

Waking from a nightmare I can't remember—
Is it the same one every night?—I hear,
when my heart has stopped pounding and I've caught my breath,
the sigh of the tideless surf not far from here.
I fumble for the light-switch. It's here somewhere.

ii.

We hear a church bell tolling
just as we cycle past
a house with a flag at half-mast,
just as a dull blast
from the limestone quarry causes
the landscape to skip a beat.

iii.

Hard by the hospital, by the narrow pathway
that led down to the harbor, stood a truncated pyramid
topped not by the caduceus but by Hermes' staff
with its twin, twined snakes. That
was the self-same symbol we saw every day,
most often backed by the red cross
decorating an amulet pinned to the breast
of the nurse who monitored your mother's morphine.
On each of the pyramid's four sides,
an image: an egg, a serpent coiled clockwise,
the serpent devouring its own tail, the serpent
coiled again, though counter-clockwise this time.
A copper plate at the pyramid's base
read *Lyss till naturen*, or *Listen to Nature*.
God knows we tried, but we heard nothing but the laughter
of gulls and the thirsty lapping of the waters.
Back at her bedside we watched the sunset
turn the entire, exemplary world
to earth, air, water, fire.

iv.

Not a sound out of your mother
save for her shallow breathing
and the bubble of oxygen
and water by her bedside.
While she went in and out
of consciousness, we sat
whispering to each other
or silent stared out through

the sick room window to
a horizon that—no doubt
this was a matter of
perspective—loomed above
the hospital, the island.
The sea was tranquil, save
for when the mainland ferry
arrived or departed, sending
wave on unnatural wave
undulating in.

v.

August sun, fair breezes. The days of summer
last, at least in relative terms, forever.
Time still passes, naturally: clouds pass over,
cloudberries ripen,

fledgling sparrows take to the air and vanish,
and the days, past Midsummer, have grown shorter.
Still, these things—days, berries, birds, clouds—are symbols,
meaning eternal.

Is this, then, the paradise I have looked for
all my days, in all I have read and written?
Is this the redeeming, the quintessential
lyrical moment?

No, since if it were I would see in the garden,
standing with the patience of lichened crosses,
all our dead, their faces like suns, their arms wide
open in welcome.

A Friend's Work

for Lynn Chandhok

Autumn comes earlier here
and I was caught off guard
when I looked up from writing
and saw out in the yard

how burdened the apple tree
is with its golden fruit,
how many already cobble
the ground around its foot,

how many, when the branches
tremble with wind or birds,
fall. Here, take this image,
translated into words:

it's summer where you are,
and nothing you can see,
I imagine, is as ready
a symbol as this tree

for how the work you've tended
for years now ripens and,
given the lightest touch,
falls into your hand.

A Ready Instrument

White curtains motionless in the still air.
Propped in the corner, strung and freshly tuned,
an old acoustic, nylon-string guitar.
Here, anytime I make the smallest sound—
cough or shift my chair, say—I can hear
the same unpicked, unfretted chord resound.

Autumn

Harvest time. The circle is complete.
Time to crush the ripened fruit for wine.
Time to grind the gathered grain for bread.

True to form, the geese pass overhead,
giving us the "V for Victory" sign
even as they beat their long retreat.

Remote

Last night I tuned that preacher in,
the one you always had to watch.
This time he wasn't cursing sin
or preaching politics and such

but telling the story of how Isaiah,
sent by the spirit of the Lord,
announces to king Hezekiah,
who's damn-near dead, that he'll be cured;

not only that, God's going to give
the king a sign to let him know
beyond a doubt he's going to live.
And not just any sign: the shadow

cast on a nearby sundial's going
to backtrack a full ten degrees;
Sure enough, it does, showing,
the preacher says (whispering like he's

revealing some great secret) how
the Lord is powerful enough
to work all kinds of wonders. *Wow,
news flash*, I thought, and nodded off.

Sometime that night I dreamed that we,
hand in hand, went for a stroll
and underneath a willow tree
found somebody's remote control.

We joked about what it was for.
I picked it up and made believe
that it controlled the willow or
the grass instead of a TV.

Weird—the grass began to sprout
like holy blazes when I pushed
fast forward; then, when I hit mute
the birds and the cicadas hushed;

and when I aimed it at the sun
and hit reverse, lo and behold:
even the sun started to run
backwards. I remote controlled

everything in the world but you.
You, when I looked around, were gone,
just like real life; all I could do
was wake up feeling twice alone

and wait there for the sun to rise
like it does every blessed day.
Vanity of vanities
I heard the television say.

The Soundman's Funeral

We honored his request, playing in lieu
of hymns or eulogies the sounds he made
    back in the old days, sounds that made
    the most unlikely tales ring true.

A squeal of brakes, a thunderclap, a shot,
a locomotive's wail, coyotes crying.
    Some of the guests by then were crying,
    others, lost in the story, not.

Rain on a tin roof, a dog barking, boughs
groaning in a great wind. We thought of him,
    of all that found its voice through him.
    A door—the front door of a house?—

slammed and we listened as someone descended
a creaking stairway, opened a car door
    started the car up, shut the door,
    then drove off. So the story ended.

Or not the story, but that episode,
to be continued anytime we hear
    one of his trademark noises, hear
    a car pull past us on the road,

say, or a dog bark. Not that he's not gone,
but it may help, now that he's left this life,
    to hear him in the sounds of life,
    which is a show, and must go on.

Visits

for my grandmother

She comes at early evening as a rule,
is there, suddenly, by the bedroom door,
a young girl seated on a wooden stool
hovering a few feet above the floor.

She looks black Irish, you say—dark hair, dark eyes,
pale skin—and wears a first communion dress.
Relative? Student? Old friend? None of these.
She visits with you often nonetheless.

She never speaks, even when spoken to.
She looks uncomfortable, you say, afraid.
Afraid for whom, though? For herself or you?
This went on for some months before you said

anything to the family, worried we
would think (as you half did) you'd lost your mind,
knowing the sighted living couldn't see
the visions you do, who are dying blind.

And sometimes they're not visions, merely a sense
the house is full of people you don't know.
The girl is one thing. These others make you tense.
We sit it out with you until they go.

One Christmas Eve, just a few miles from here,
choked with pneumonia, your mother died.
Delirious with fever and with fear,
she cast around and called out names and cried,

until—it hits me now, how brave you were—
you climbed into the bed and held her tight
and stroked her silver hair and sang to her.
I think of this, sitting with you tonight.

You touch my arm with one hand, with the other
present to me a person of thin air.
Bill, I don't believe you've met my mother.
I don't doubt for a moment she is there.

Pacific

It wasn't always single malts for me.
I can remember one time in the navy
some of us were so desperate for a drink,
we broke into the ship's infirmary,
took the rubbing alcohol, and mixed it
with grapefruit juice. Like greyhounds, but with very,
very bad vodka. Jesus, that was a party.
But we were careful. We filled all the bottles
with water, so you couldn't tell from looking,
and even if you took the covers off
and sniffed them, they still smelled like alcohol.
Of course, the hangover was pretty vicious,
and even worse, next morning, bright and early,
all the crew were ordered up on deck.
At first we thought they'd found out what we'd done.
And as we stood there on the cruiser's deck,
sweltering in the Pacific sun,
shaking, ready to puke, I tell you, I
was ready to confess and end the torture.
After a while, though, it was clear the captain
didn't have a clue about our party.
No, he was going on about how the islands
where we were going were crawling with diseases,
and that we'd need to get inoculated.
And then I noticed the ship's doctor there,

looking like a waiter with his tray
of vaccine, and a few syringes and—
Christ, I felt like crying—the same bottles
of alcohol we'd emptied and refilled.
What could we do? We stood there sweating, praying
nobody in the crew had anything
incurable, and took our shots from needles
the doctor wiped off once—quickly—with water
after he'd just stuck the guy beside us.
We lived. By which I mean we all survived
that little cock-up. I'm the only one,
though, of the five of us that threw that party
who made it back alive from the Pacific.
Before that mess was over I saw men
more desperate for a drink than even we'd been,
guys who were in the first boats going in,
who knew as sure as they knew they were living
that they were going to die there on that beach
or somewhere in the water short of it:
Anything they could think of they would drink—
paint-thinner, aftershave, it didn't matter,
so long as it would get them good and numb.
Guys would drink Aqua Velva from the bottle.
Remember those commercials they ran later?
There's something about an Aqua Velva man?
The happiest day of my entire life,
happier, even, than my wedding day,
happier than the days our kids were born,
the happiest day of my entire life
was when we dropped the bomb on Hiroshima.
I get these looks of shock from younger people
when I say things like that, but they don't know.
That's good. I hope they never understand.

It wasn't always single malt for me.
Now it is, when I drink, which isn't often—
it's just, today I've got a wake to go to,
for Jimmy, Margaret's brother. He was under
MacArthur, helped retake the Philippines.
Neither of us could stand wakes. We'd both seen
enough dead bodies in the war to last
a lifetime—that's how Jimmy always put it—
and anytime that Margaret didn't force us,
anytime it wasn't someone close,
we would play cards or golf or see a movie.
And when we had to go, we'd go together.
First, though, we'd stop off someplace for a drink.
Margaret's not happy that I'm here, she thinks
I should be at the funeral home already,
not doing anything, just being there,
supporting her. And probably she's right—
He was her only brother, and I'm her husband,
and husbands have a duty to be strong.
My only consolation is that Jimmy,
Jimmy would understand the way it hits me,
thinking about him lying in a coffin:
He'd understand I need a shot of courage.

Post-Colonial Studies

Australia

The two surviving
speakers of Mati Ke, ancient
sister and brother,
honor a tribal taboo
and do not speak to each other.

Fiji

On an island bought
for him by a worthy follower,
Adi Da Samraj,
long awaited avatar,
native New Yorker, holds sway.

Laos

In the country, homes
are often set on stilts. Some
of the stilts are bombs,
ordinance left from the war.
Some of the bombs are still live.

Improvisation

So-and-so must be spinning in the grave
we say when something we think so-and-so
would have been horrified by happens, though
common sense tells us most don't have the room
to actually rotate in the tomb.
Even the more exalted ones who have
a mausoleum in which they might turn
are cooped up in a coffin or an urn.
Lenin, on learning that the Soviet state
had fallen, was undoubtedly irate
but couldn't, I imagine, do much more
than rattle the glass showcase where he lies
while guards and pilgrims drew back in surprise.
Nobody in the grave, or very few,
actually spins the way we say they do.
Think of the possibilities, though, the power,
if they had room enough to spin and we
could somehow harness them for energy,
rig them like turbines, say, then do or say
just the wrong thing and let them twirl away
in gothic, industrial caves under the earth.
Then our betrayals of all for which they stood
might turn, as they turned, to some current good,
and they bequeath us something of real worth.

On a Phrase of Thomas Merton's

the dank weather of Nazism

It has been raining for a thousand years.
Mold and moss and mushroom fructify.
How long, we wonder, till the weather clears?

Nobody in authority appears
to know, nor will they speculate as to why
it has been raining for a thousand years.

Underground sources, though, say these are tears
the ghosts of other, long-dead, races cry.
How long, we wonder, till the weather clears?

Not that we worry, really. Our engineers
have raised up walls unfathomably high.
It has been raining for a thousand years,

a steady drizzle, a whisper in our ears
bidding us despair, despair and die.
How long, we wonder, till the weather clears?

Panicked reports come in from the frontiers.
The walls are crumbling, they say. The end is nigh.
It has been raining for a thousand years.
How long, we wonder, till the weather clears?

Requiem for a Returnee

from the Swedish of Håkan Sandell

Czeslaw Milosz has moved to Krakow
I heard from his Swedish translator yesterday,
to draw in with a deep rattling breath
the concrete dust by the building scaffolds,
breathed out again as the muse speaks her last.
And yet it seems like the scene of his death
should have remained a California
of perfected loss, peeled, wide open,
trembling with desert heat and alienation,
a well-aged alienation, where not the Beach Boys
but Chopin, Brahms, and Shostakovich
are played at the cultivated funeral.
Nicely-built young American female
poets would have sparkled in the backmost benches
hour-glass shaped after a lifetime of salads
elegant too in the most stylish clothing
with small threads of cotton over their shoulders
in that self-satisfied self-preoccupation
I too will adopt any day now
in order to claim my feminine rights.
Paler, now, after the warnings about skin cancer
for over two decades leanly writing
for no one but themselves or no one

but their lovely, gold-framed reflections.
So cool in spite of the heat, and sexy
like they would be if all of the men had died out
and they were sexy only for themselves and
for the shelves in the lesbian bookstore.
Poets, yes, but more like muses
for fate, music, and watercolor painting.
Muses for sports cars, for the streetlights'
mildness in the dusk, for the blue of the waves
and of the neon letters high as falcons,
they all of them seem to be the bearers of a peculiar
bittersweet inspiration with no one to receive it.
Oh Sappho, California, sweet music,
why does Czeslaw Milosz travel to Krakow,
only, at the birth of his country, to die
like an utterly ordinary grey old man
when the long beaches' mummifying heat
and a sea as blue as a white cat's eye
made a background suited to a Greek god,
youthful in jeans and drunk on exile
like Odysseus' men on milk-sweet lotus?

Contra Dante (Kind of)

Forget about the Beatific Vision.
Not that it's not impressive in its glory
and worthy of a god in God's position,

but if I make it to Mount Purgatory
(and yes, that's one big "if," I realize)
and trudge my way up story after story

I'll settle in the Earthly Paradise
located at the top, it being more,
well, earthly, which is better in my eyes.

Earthly perfection's what I'm looking for:
the world I know, more or less as I know it,
prolonged, minus the death and pain and gore

(hard to imagine, maybe, but read the poet
Isaiah on the lion and the lamb).
If I found that, there's no way I'd outgrow it,

even if I grew holier than I am
(not *the* I AM, but I as I am now).
Can I be honest? I don't give a damn

if I miss most of the celestial show
(it will go on like clockwork whether I
am there or not) so long as far below

(which, from where I stand now, is still on high)
I can sit down under an actual tree
on actual grass beneath an actual sky

of blue that as it drops back lets me see
the southern constellations overhead.
That would be more than good enough for me,

enough to make me not mind being dead.
And if a Beatrice came from above
to take me heavenwards, I'd try instead

to tell her *she* should be the one to move.
She'd hem, she'd haw, I'd bring her flowers and rhyme,
I'd say, "Stay here with me and be my love,

seeing we now have world enough and time."

Kolmården Zoo

Over our heads, trailing a wake of air
and an enormous shadow as it passed,
the falcon glided to its trainer's fist
and settled like a loaded weapon there.

Then, while she fed the bird bit after bit
of . . . what? Rabbit? The trainer gave her talk:
These birds, she said, prey on the small and weak,
adding for the children's benefit

that this, though it seems cruel, is really good
since otherwise the other rabbits, mice,
squirrels, what have you, would run out of space
and die of illness or a lack of food.

I know what she was trying to get across,
and I don't doubt it would be healthier
if we were more familiar than we are
with how the natural world draws life from loss;

and granted, nothing is more natural
than death incarnate falling from the sky;
and granted, it is better some should die,
however agonizingly, than all.

Still, to teach children this is how things go
is one thing, to insist that it is good
is something else—almost to make a god
of this unsatisfactory status quo,

this vicious circle that the clock hands draw
and quarter, while the serpent bites its tail,
or eats the dust, or strikes at someone's heel,
or winds up comprehended by a claw.

She launched the bird again. We watched it climb
out of the amphitheatre, headed toward
the darkened spires of a nearby wood,
then bank, then angle toward us one last time.

The Moons of Earth

Earth, despite all the astronomers say, has not one moon but many.
All save the one called the Moon are inhabited, all have distinctive,
frankly fantastical climates and landscapes. Initiates know this,
meteorologists, farmers, sportsmen and almanac keepers
know what was once, in the antediluvian world, common knowledge.
They have conspired for six thousand years, now, to keep it a secret,
fearing that we, if we knew of inhabited worlds in near orbit,
might be so taken with them we'd neglect our terrestrial business.
And they are right. Having unearthed their secret I've found myself
        growing
arrogant, distant, bored with the every day details of living,
pale and exhausted from gazing all night at the heavens. Oh stranger,
stranger whom I, both by chance and design, entrust with the secret,
do not take lightly my warning; do not believe for a moment
you can believe in such things without gradually growing inhuman.
Think of the Harvest Moon, patchworked with wheatfields, orchards
        and vineyards;
think of the Hunter's Moon, teeming with prey unafraid of the arrow;
think of the Hunger Moon, peopled by figures from Giacometti;
think of the Flower Moon, the Ice Moon, the Strawberry Moon and
        the others.
You, if you ever return to your life, will return as a stranger.

Nightingale

Muse of musicians and poets
whose song is taken to be
song itself, how is it
such melody

originates in a creature
whose name, read word for word,
is a hard time to weather
for any bird?

What does the shutters' rattling,
what does the night wind's wail
have to do with your music,
Night in Gale?

By what Hermetic method
is a nocturnal storm
incorporated into
your twilit form;

by what unconscious measure
tuned to the song that I
am here in hopes of hearing
by and by?

Aubade

On a dead street
in a high wall
a wooden gate
I don't recall

ever seeing open
is today
and I who happen
to pass this way

in passing glimpse
a garden lit
by dark lamps
at the heart of it.

Bill Coyle's poems have appeared widely in magazines and anthologies, including *The Hudson Review*, *The New Criterion*, *The New Republic*, and *Poetry*. He is a translator from the Swedish, and his versions of the poet Håkan Sandell have appeared in *PN Review* and *Ars Interpres* and are forthcoming in the anthology *The Other Side of Landscape*. Mr. Coyle teaches in the English Department at Salem State College in Salem, Massachusetts. He lives in Somerville, Massachusetts.

The New Criterion is recognized as one of the foremost contemporary venues for poetry with a regard for traditional meter and form. The magazine was thus an early leader in that poetic renaissance that has come to be called the New Formalism. Building upon its commitment to serious poetry, *The New Criterion* in 2000 established an annual prize, which carries an award of $3000. Bill Coyle is the sixth winner.